PRESENTATION

SKILLS

Suzy Siddons

Suzy Siddons is a professional trainer who, over the last 15 years, has specialised in (among other things) communication and presentation training. She has run more than 500 training courses and workshops on these subjects, and has experience in both television and radio broadcasting. She runs her own training company, Chapterhouse Training Services, which provides training to many leading companies. She is the author of several business books, including *Delivering Training* (1997), part of the IPD's Training Essentials series.

TRAINING EXTRAS is a comprehensive series covering all the crucial management skill areas. Each booklet includes the key issues, helpful starting points, and practical advice in a concise and lively style. Together, they form an accessible library reflecting current best practice – ideal for study or quick reference.

Other titles in the series include:

The Institute of Personnel and Development is the leading publisher of books and reports for personnel and training professionals and students and for all those concerned with the effective management and development of people at work. For full details of all our titles please telephone the Publishing Department on 0181 263 3387.

PRESENTATION
SKILLS

Suzy Siddons

INSTITUTE OF PERSONNEL AND DEVELOPMENT

Design and typesetting by Paperweight
Printed in Great Britain by
Short Run Press, Exeter

British Library Cataloguing in Publication Data
A catalogue record for this book is available from the
British Library

ISBN
0-85292-743-6

The views expressed in this book are the author's own and
may not necessarily reflect those of the IPD.

INSTITUTE OF PERSONNEL
AND DEVELOPMENT

IPD House, Camp Road, London SW19 4UX
Tel.: 0181 971 9000   Fax: 0181 263 3333
Registered Charity No. 1038333.
A company limited by guarantee. Registered in England No. 2931892.
Registered office as above.

 # Contents

Acknowledgements

I would like to thank my husband, David Nickson, for all his help and input; my cat, Bonzo, for inspiring me; and, not least, Anne Cordwent, the commissioning editor without whom...

1

Why Give Presentations at All?

I do not object to people looking at their watches when I am speaking. But I strongly object when they start shaking them to make sure they are still going.

Lord Birkett (1883–1962) (attributed)

Introduction

A good presentation contains many of the same constituents as a good restaurant meal. The participants should be hungry. The chef should be at least competent, if not inspired. The menu should be tempting, understandable and offer a range of choices to all the diners. The ingredients should be the best possible. The service should be impeccable. The ambiance should be comfortable and attractive. There should be no nasty after-effects; and it is helpful to know the location of the restaurant and when people are expected to arrive.

The most important factor in the success of both a meal and a presentation is the attitude of the consumers. Just as you cannot force people to eat something that they neither like nor need, so you should never force-feed an audience with indigestible, unnecessary, uninteresting or irrelevant information. The audience's attitudes, responses, reactions and needs throughout the presentation are of paramount importance. In fact, without an audience you have no presentation.

This is what this book is all about: how to give presentations that serve genuine business needs, as well as how to make each and every one of them enjoyable, interesting, stimulating, memorable and value for money.

Are presentations worth the effort?

It may seem strange to begin a book on presentation skills by questioning the very need for presentations at all. This questioning is, however, something that is either never done or not done rigorously enough. All too often we deliver presentations without thinking through the genuine benefits that this particular method of passing information to others should bring, let alone concerning ourselves with what the audience want to gain.

An expensive way to get your message across

If you average out the value of a well-paid business person's time, you come to a figure of around about £1 per minute. This means that an audience of 20, spending an hour listening to a presentation, will use £1,200 worth of time that could have been otherwise spent selling, manufacturing marketable products, servicing the client base or helping the business to run profitably. If you then add up all the time that business people spend in presentations (often up to four hours a week), you get to a startling figure of thousands of pounds a year *for each person*. It therefore follows that any presentation you give had better be worth the cost of the audience's time, not to mention the time that you as the presenter have spent in preparing it, delivering it and following it up.

Why give presentations?

Why do we give presentations at all, bearing in mind how extraordinarily expensive in terms of time and effort they are? Table 1 sets out the reasons for either giving or choosing not to give one.

Table 1
REASONS FOR AND AGAINST PRESENTATIONS

Reasons for	Reasons against
• You need to communicate time-critical information to a large group of people.	• We always have presentations on Thursdays.
• You have to persuade an audience to make a choice, change their mind, take a set of actions or pass on information to others, and you need to do it *in person*.	• The information you are giving is in fact already known to the audience and the presentation neither re-interprets it nor puts it into a new context.
• The audience are interested, concerned or need to hear what you are going to say.	• The audience are not interested in what you are going to say, or do not need to hear it.
• You have to teach skills or give information cost effectively to more than three or four people at a time.	• The *audience* do not know why they are there, or *you* are not sure why *you* are presenting.
• You have a clear set of objectives for the presentation.	• You have no objectives for the presentation.

You should consider several major factors before starting to spend any time on preparing a presentation. Ask yourself the following questions:

- Could I get this information across in a more effective manner? Might it be possible to use e-mail, a report, a short meeting, a conference call or some other method of communication?
- Have I got the time and energy to prepare the presentation properly?
- How much will the presentation cost – and, at that price, is it likely to be cost-effective?
- What is the presentation for? What do I want the audience to do *after* they have heard the presentation?

If the answers are 'Yes', 'No', 'Too much' and 'No idea' to the questions above, then you should seriously consider whether a presentation really is the best method in the first place. If you think about all the presentations you have sat through in your career, I wonder whether you could honestly say that every one of them was worth the time and effort involved.

So, is there a perfect recipe for a presentation? Can a presenter realistically expect to please all the people all the time? Of course not. What an effective presenter *can* expect to do, however, is to put the message across in a way that involves the audience both intrinsically (by making them react, think, and compare) and extrinsically (by making them discuss, find out more, or take certain courses of action). An effective presenter can also expect to leave each member of the audience feeling that they have learned something that is of use to them, and to have done so in a way that both made the information real to them personally and also left them with a clear sense of what the next step ought to be.

Of course, the presenter cannot do this without knowing a considerable amount about the people who are going to make up the audience. It is to this topic that we now turn.

2

Selecting Your Subject, Researching Your Audience

> It is the admirer and the watcher who provoke us to all the insanities we commit.
>
> Seneca (ca 4 BC–ca AD 65)

When you decide to give a presentation, you usually have a fair idea of what it is that you are going to present. Usually your subject has already been defined, either by yourself or by the people who want you to give the presentation. This then leaves you with the knotty problem of exactly what, and how much, to tell your audience. Sometimes this appears to be obvious, such as when you are asked to present financial accounts or sales figures, but even here you have to decide whether you are just going to present the bald facts or whether in addition you are going to interpret that information in any way. It is fair to say that any presentation, no matter how simple it may seem, can be done in many, many different ways. But for any presentation to be effective, it must positively interest the listeners. This fact alone means that the audience, and not the presentation itself, is your starting-point.

To take an example, think about presenting a new product. The sort of presentation that you would give to the sales people who are going to sell the product, the presentation that you would give to the service force who are going to support the product, and the presentation that you would give to an actual customer who is going to buy and use the product would each have to be very different – even though some of the same facts would be covered.

Generally speaking, your audience's needs will fall into seven main areas:

- straightforward information (specifications, figures, results)
- historical background (to increase the audience's understanding of the present situation)
- comparisons (to allow them to choose between products, services or actions)

- interpretation (of what the facts mean to each of them personally)
- motivation (to take a certain set of actions or decisions)
- education (how to do something well or better)
- entertainment.

In the case of the product presentation, the prime needs of the sales people would be information, history, comparison, motivation (to sell) and interpretation, whereas the prime needs of the service force would be information and education, and the needs of the customers would be motivation (to buy), comparison, interpretation and information.

Researching your audience

What do you need to know about your audience before you start to prepare your presentation? There are four areas that you should consider:

- the audience's objectives – the reasons they have come
- the level of the audience's knowledge of the subject you are presenting
- the history of the relationship between you the presenter (and your company) and the audience
- how the audience prefer to assimilate information.

The audience's objectives

These are often closely tied to their job. Are they there to sell or to buy? Are they concerned with the financial side of business or with marketing strategy? Is their role a technical one or are they concerned with 'people' issues? What are they going to do with the information you are presenting, and which aspect of it is likely to interest them most?

The audience's existing knowledge

Always be careful of jargon and industry-specific phraseology. Jargon is a useful shorthand if you all know what it means, but if *anyone* in the audience does not understand the acronyms or specialist terms you are using, then you are wasting that person's time. Always define jargon the first time you use it.

How much background will the audience need? If you are aware that they know very little about your subject, would it be wise for you to include a glossary of terms, an overview or an introduction to the subject? If, on the other hand, they already know a great deal about your subject, why are they there? Are they expecting a new interpretation of what they know, or are you going just to waste their time by reiterating old facts?

The history of the relationship between you and the audience

It is easy to overlook this. I remember once giving a presentation about a new computer program to a company that I had never dealt with before, although the company that I was working for had dealt with them for many years. The presentation seemed to go well but, when it came to question time, every single question was about delivery times and help-line support – and most of those questions were hostile. It was not until later that I discovered that my own company had in the recent past let my audience's company down badly over both those factors. If I had known that, I would have adapted the presentation so as to reassure my audience of the utter reliability of our deliveries and the excellence of the newly trained help-desk staff.

It takes only a few minutes to find out whether people in the audience know of any problems that might affect the presentation – and it is well worth the effort. If you are in doubt, ring up one or two of the proposed audience and simply ask whether they have any worries or concerns that you should know about.

How the audience prefer to assimilate new information

If we were all the same, the world would be an easier (if duller) place for presenters. In reality, though, we all have different preferences. As presenters, our own style of delivery is based on the way that we as individuals like to behave, and as members of an audience we also have preferences for certain ways of receiving information.

My favourite presenters, for example, like to talk about the whole picture; they like to show how this new information is going to affect the audience personally; they like to get on with things, avoiding getting too concerned with the detail; and they include lots of anecdotes and examples. I could listen to them for hours. However, I have a colleague who really dislikes this sort of presenter, who thinks that they should pay more attention to detail, should include more hard facts, and who is not in the least interested in anecdotes. In short, this colleague considers anything that is not totally factual a waste of time. Quite often we both go to the same presentation but come away feeling very differently about how it went.

It is extremely likely that you are going to encounter a mix of personal likes and dislikes in any audience, and that many of these will not match the way that you prefer to present. This is where you have to put yourself in the audience's shoes and cater for their tastes as well as your own. Although it is not possible to be all things to all people, there are nonetheless some general pointers that may help you to avoid irritating large numbers of any audience that you speak to. So here are some of the habits that presenters must avoid:

- Not putting in enough detail for the people who like to collect facts. Solve this by distributing a handout with all the relevant details at the end of the presentation.

- Putting in so much detail that half the audience is bored to death. Solve this by using the 'So what?' test: if you can ask 'So what?' about a particular piece of information, and find no good answer, then it should not be in.

- Concentrating too much on the personal side of what you are saying. Cure this by having summary slides of the hard facts (financial data, time-scales, performance factors, legal and material implications, etc).

- Concentrating too little on the personal implications of what you are saying. Cure this by including a phrase or two for each main point that explains how it will affect the way in which people work.

Adapting your presentation in this manner does not mean that you have to be a chameleon or abandon your personal style; it just requires you to make allowances for other people's priorities, particularly when they are different from yours.

Having thoroughly researched your audience and defined exactly what they and you want out of the presentation, you now have to begin preparing your script.

3

Writing the Script and Preparing the Cue Cards

> The secret of being a bore is to tell everything.
>
> Voltaire (1694–1778)

Gathering your ideas

Experienced presenters each have their own preferred method of preparing their scripts, so if you have a system that works for you, stick with it. However, for those who are completely new to script-writing, here are some pointers.

You have already decided the subject and purpose of your presentation; now you need to collect together the information that will make up the bulk of the content. Use a pad of adhesive Post-It™ notes and write the points down on them – one per note. You need use only key words at this stage, because the first step in preparing a script is simply to get the ideas into a prioritised and logical order. Using moveable notes allows you to experiment with the order in which you are going to present your points, whereas making a list tends to create an arbitrary priority which may limit your creativity.

Gather the points into logical groups and decide which require examples to make them clear and which will need a visual aid to clarify their meaning. Work out how you are going to link the groups of information together. (Using the phrase 'So this means that…' should get your mind working along the right lines.)

Now you need to define your key messages: these are the ones that the audience will (hopefully) take away with them. You need to expand these ideas and find at least three ways of driving their importance home. There is a good reason for repeating the key messages three times: that is how long it takes for your audience to digest and begin to remember what you have said. This does not mean that you should say the same thing three times – which would be tedious – but that you need to make your point, illustrate it in some way with an example or a visual aid, add a statement explaining the benefit for the audience and then summarise what you have said.

Let's take an example: imagine you are giving a sales presentation about a new financial product – a pension plan. One of your key messages is that this particular plan allows customers to 'take a holiday' from regular payments for six months if they should lose their job. The plan you are selling allows customers to do this without endangering their entire pension. So, you might say something like this:

> One of the strongest benefits of this plan is the protection it allows you in the event you lose your job and find it impossible to pay the pension instalments (*key statement*).

> For example, someone paying £200 each month could take a six-month 'holiday' from the plan, thus freeing up £1,200 at a time when money would be scarce (*example*).

> Almost all other pension plans do not allow this: a six-month gap with such plans would threaten your entire pension. Not so with our plan: you have the safety cushion of a six-month gap while you find another job (*benefit*).

You would then reinforce this message at the end of the presentation by mentioning it again in your summary.

Go through all the key points and structure them in the same way. You now have the bones of the presentation and can begin to piece the whole thing together.

Scripting considerations

Some people like to write out the whole presentation and then condense the script onto cue cards; others like to write down just the bullet points and make brief notes to remind themselves of the examples and evidence they are going to use. Whichever way suits you best is fine, but a word of warning: reading a script verbatim sounds artificial and stilted, and may well take some of your credibility away. The written word and the spoken word are simply not the same – and the audience will recognise this. If you do not know your subject well enough to be able to talk about it without a word-for-word script, then maybe you should not be giving the presentation at all. Cue cards are there as an *aide-mémoire* – something to keep you on track and ensure that you make all the points you want to make. A rehearsal will help you to fix your main points in your mind much more clearly than a full and detailed script (see below).

Presentation structure

There are three stages to a presentation: the *introduction*, the *main body* and the *close* (note that this structure makes it easy to reinforce the information at least three times).

The introduction

Here you need to set the scene, establish expectations, gain credibility, catch the audience's interest, make them listen actively, and clearly point to your conclusion (but not necessarily in any particular order).

Scene-setting is vital at the start of a presentation. The audience may have preconceived ideas about your subject that may be false; they may expect you to cover points that are not relevant; they may not know the background of or reasons for the presentation. You need to 'frame up' what you are going to be talking about and set the presentation in its proper context.

This is where a title for the presentation is very useful. Prepare a slide showing the presentation title (and possibly a subtitle as well), your name, job title and the location. This should be the very first visual aid you use. Titles should do much more than just state the presentation subject. They can be used for setting the tone of the presentation, showing that you understand the audience's concerns and providing a theme.

For example, let's say that you are preparing a presentation on a new computer graphics program called 'Draw It All'. The presentation is to an audience of railway engineers. You could simply entitle the presentation 'Draw It All Software' – but what an opportunity you would have missed! Think again. A title like

> A graphics program that would have excited Isambard Kingdom Brunel

with a subtitle

> 'Draw It All' will keep you on track

says much more and sets the expectation of a presentation about a product that is tailored to the real needs of the audience.

Because it is at the start of a presentation that the audience makes its mind up whether to believe you or not, you need to gain credibility by explaining to them exactly why *you personally* are giving this presentation. Are you an expert? Is the subject of the presentation something you have in-depth knowledge about? Are you the representative of a recognised body? Don't be shy: audiences are much more likely to believe the truth of what you are saying if you state your expertise up front.

At the start of any presentation you need to set the audience's expectations clearly. How long are you going to take? Will they have the opportunity to ask questions at the end? Is anyone else involved in the presentation? Will they need to take notes, or do you have a hand-out for them? What is the agenda? You must make these things clear so that the audience can settle back comfortably, knowing just what to expect.

Active listening on the part of the audience is particularly important if you want people to remember your messages (which of course you do). Audiences listen actively if they are waiting for information that they feel they need, or are hearing information that directly applies to them. A cold recital of facts with no attempt to interpret them in the audience's terms will be neither memorable nor even interesting. To encourage active listening you must show that you understand what the audience want and need.

For example, imagine giving a presentation to the finance division of a large company about a new computer-plus-software package that will allow them to complete their monthly, quarterly and yearly accounts 50 per cent faster than they do at present. Would these people really be interested in the internal mechanics of the computer (the processor speed, the disk capacity and the technical details of how the computer works) or would they be much more concerned with the amount of time it will take to learn the new program, the number of people who can work on the same program at once, and whether the program can calculate VAT and PAYE automatically?

Facts are not of themselves important to most of us. We need to have them interpreted: to be told what they mean and how they apply to us. Here is an example:

Fact: 64 megabytes of memory.

What this means: system is large enough to run word-processing, spreadsheets and graphics programs simultaneously.

How it benefits us: you do not have to close down one program before opening another. In short, you save time. You can have two programs running on screen at the same time and can switch from one to the other quickly. This facility allows you to look simultaneously at a written report and a spreadsheet or graphics package.

Right from the start of the presentation the audience should be aware that the information you are telling them relates to their reality and that you have made the effort to think about their needs. Even if you have a mixed audience with a range of different concerns, you should signal up front that there will be something for everyone.

By clearly pointing to your conclusion at the start of the presentation you achieve two important things: you reinforce the main message (people remember more clearly the first pieces of information they hear than the later ones) and you keep the presentation on track. Everything you say after this will lead to the same conclusion and add veracity to your arguments. Don't save your main message for the end: the audience need to know where the presentation is going.

The main body

This is where you flesh out your main points. You give examples of what you are talking about; you show, if necessary, why and how you have come to the conclusions you have; you give references that will help convince the audience of the truth of what you are saying; and you explain some of the more important points in greater detail.

There is a golden rule here: don't go into so much detail that you overload the audience. Our brains are not very good at remembering everything we hear. By contrast, we remember a great deal more of what we see or feel, and most of what we actually do or discuss. The presenter should bear this in mind and, as far as possible, illustrate the more important points *visually*. By that I do not mean putting up endless slides with the same words on them as the ones we are speaking. That's lazy and ineffective. Use the slides instead to cast more light on what you are saying through the use of diagrams, flow charts, photographs, graphics and cartoons.

All presentations should also encourage questions and discussion, because that is when the audience have the chance to articulate what they have learned from the presentation.

The close

A weak ending to a presentation can undo all the good that the first two parts have done. There is usually a feeling of relief that sweeps over us (and sometimes the audience!) when we realise that we are nearing the end of the presentation – and this can lead to carelessness. It is at this point that we really need to keep control of ourselves and the presentation. Its close should round off the facts you have presented with a summary that reinforces the key points that have been made. But this summary should not be a mere recital of the agenda:

> So, I've talked about the new car we are introducing to the market, its performance, the extras that you can have and the options available for delivery...

It should instead be a clear and punchy review of the important facts that you feel the audience should remember:

> The Lomotilia 7 Sports Coupé is one of the few race-performance cars on the road today, available in 16 colours, with real leather upholstery, mobile phone, CD and radio. It has optional satellite navigation, air-conditioned seats and a removable roof. Production is under way and delivery will be less than three years after your orders are placed.

You then need to give a 'call to action': in other words, tell your listeners what you want them to do next. This may be a simple request for questions or something more complex, such as asking the audience to make a set of difficult decisions. Either way, there should be a call to action of some sort. Even in a short presentation reporting, for example, on the progress of a project or updating the audience on the way in which the office is being run should put people back into the real world where they can use the information that you have given them.

Finally, you need to make sure that everyone knows where to contact you and also the correct spelling of your name (an important consideration in these days of the Internet and e-mail).

Being yourself and using humour

The best presenters are always themselves – only more so. 'Yourself with the volume turned up,' as a friend of mine puts it.

It is unwise to pretend that you are a limelight-loving extrovert with a flair for oratory if in fact you are a rather reticent person who, although enthusiastic about the given subject, prefers to be exact and a little understated. It is just as unwise to try to curb a natural tendency towards flamboyance by reining yourself in tightly in order to look composed. The real you will always creep out. If your natural style is to tell jokes, or if you have an ironic or even sardonic way of looking at things, let it show; but if you feel in any way uncomfortable using humour or irony, then leave it alone. Present in the same way that you normally go about things, only more so – a little louder, a little more expansive, and always being aware that the audience must be able to hear you clearly.

Creating rapport with the audience

At the start of a presentation you need to create rapport with the audience. Rapport may be defined as:

- reference
- relationship
- connection
- correspondence.

This is exactly what you must show clearly from the moment you begin your presentation.

Refer to people in the audience at regular intervals either individually by their own name or collectively by their company's name. Make a good deal of eye contact with them, and make all your gestures towards them. Mention their personal expertise. Never talk down to them: just as you may know several things that they may not, they will certainly know a great amount that you will not. Wherever you have something in common with the audience, mention it. You are not there to blind them with your expertise but to persuade them that, together, you and they can solve a problem, supply a service, reach a decision and make things work better – or whatever it is that you are trying to achieve with the presentation.

Prompts

It is almost certain that the first time you present a particular subject you will need some kind of prompt to help you through the presentation. There are many ways of doing this. Here are three of the simpler options: cue cards, notes on sheets of paper and overhead projector slide frames. Each has its advantages and disadvantages.

Cue cards

Use 5in. × 3in. record cards. Drill a hole through one corner of them and link them together with a treasury tag or a ring. Number each card. That way, even if you drop them they will still be together and it will be easy to find your place again.

Write the subject matter at the top of each card. Underneath that jot down the main points that you are going to cover, the link to the next subject and the number of any slides you are going to use.

The advantages of using cue cards are that they are fairly small (so you cannot hide behind them!) and that if your hands tremble with nerves the cards do not rustle. They also give you something to hold onto, which means that you can keep your hands above your waist in a natural way. The disadvantage is that you may find you have a tendency to make your writing so small that you have to peer at the cards to decipher what you have written.

Notes on paper

Again, number each page and put them in a ringbinder. (This makes them easy to turn over.) Write down the subject at the top of the sheet; put the key points below that, along with the numbers of each slide. Again, write down the links between each subject.

Notes have the advantages of saving you the trouble of transferring your points to cue cards and of allowing you to go into more detail (but not too much, please!). The disadvantages of notes are that if you do not have a lectern you will have to hold them in front of you, which hides part of you from the audience, and that if you are nervous the sheets can rustle alarmingly, distracting the audience from what you are trying to get across.

Slide frames

These are the white 'wings' that fold out from the sides of the clear transparent folder into which you put the overhead projector slides. They have a write-on wipe-off surface that allows you to put key points and examples onto them. Their advantage is that you can glance down at the overhead projector and see at once the points you need to make that are associated with each slide. The disadvantage is that there is not a lot of room on them, so again you are forced to make your handwriting tiny, which obviously makes it hard to read.

Whichever method you choose, try not to overload your prompt materials by putting too much on them. If you spend the entire time peering down at them you will lose touch with the audience and defeat the purpose of the presentation. Remember: you should be communicating with the audience – not your *aides-mémoire*.

Visual aids and back-up materials

You have a wide variety of back-up materials from which to choose – from the simple flip chart, overhead projector or poster, to the more sophisticated computer-generated slides, to video and multimedia presentation software. I do not have room to cover each of these individually, so the points given here have general application.

Why bother?

Why bother using visual aids at all? Surely we can make our presentations so vivid that our words will linger in the audience's memory long after the presentation is over? Not so! As I mentioned before, just hearing something is not enough to create strong memories. We need to involve as many of the audience's senses as possible to drive our messages home.

It is an undeniable fact that our visual memory is very much sharper than our aural memory (except for things such as music and rhythm), so using pictures and diagrams will genuinely help the audience to understand and internalise the messages we send. It is also true that a long and wordy description of an object is not nearly as effective as a photograph, or indeed the actual object itself, no matter how cleverly we pick our words.

Effective images

Here is a set of rules to make your visual aids effective:

- *Keep them simple*. Just as you can overload your audience with facts, so you can overload them with complex images. If you are forced to present a really complex image, try to build it up piece by piece.

- *Explain what the audience will be looking at*. Describe each image *before* you show it. You might say, for example, 'The next slide shows the layout of the factory floor. At the top right-hand corner you will be able to see assembly line one...'

- *Use colour wherever possible*. Colour in itself wakes the brain up; more specifically, it can highlight important parts of the slide (but be careful with the use of red on slides concerning money!).

- *Ensure that any lettering on slides can be read from the back of the audience*. What may be perfectly plain to you (being nearer to the screen than anyone else in the room) may be far too small for the people at the back.

- *Always have a slide illustrating spatial information*. That is to say, have slides showing how things are laid out and how they fit together. Maps and plans are extremely difficult to explain with words alone.

- *Always illustrate numerical information*. Most people find numbers hard to remember. Also, if possible, show what the numbers mean by using bar charts, pie charts and line graphs.

Finally – as if it needs saying – *don't stand in front of the screen*!

Handout material

There are bound to be people in your audience who will want back-up material, either because they need more detail than the presentation has contained or because they need to pass your message on to others. Make these available *after* the presentation; if you give them out before, there is a tendency for the audience to read the handout and not pay attention to what you are saying. What's more, the intermittent rustling and flapping of paper will drive you mad.

Fine tuning your presentation

Your presentation is now prepared, the slides are ready and you yourself are ready for the next stage: the rehearsal. But before you do this you need to stand back from all that hard work and look through your presentation as if *you* were the audience. What needs clarifying? Why is each piece of information included? Is your conclusion clear and compelling? Are all the visual aids necessary? Does the presentation consider the audience's needs throughout?

Ask yourself these questions and, if there is any doubt, go back and edit again. Less is usually more in the case of most presentations, so cut out any extraneous information that does not truly add to your message.

When all this has been done, you are set for the next stage: rehearsal.

4

Rehearsal, Voice and Delivery (and a Word about Nerves)

Ivry gr-reat orator ought to be accompanied by an orchesthry or, at worst, a pianist who would play trills while th'artist was refreshin' himself with a glass iv iced wather.

Finley Peter Dunne (1867–1936)

Rehearsal

This word conjures up the image of a theatre director and wardrobe mistress scurrying around the stage while an actor endlessly repeats his or her lines, doesn't it? Well, to a certain extent this is what needs to happen, except that you are theatre director and wardrobe mistress all in one.

Why do we need to rehearse? The sad fact is that the very first time we articulate anything – be it instructions on how to get to our house or a formal presentation of the yearly figures for our business – we are the first person to hear those words. Very often the words and phrases that come out of our mouths are as much a surprise to ourselves as they are to anyone else listening. We then immediately go into edit mode, thinking, 'No, that isn't what I meant to say at all...' and then start to correct ourselves. What started off as a crystal-clear thought becomes a series of 'ums', 'ers' and hesitations while we frantically search for the right words. The only way to cure this sorry state of affairs is to rehearse.

Rehearsals serve many purposes

The great advantage of rehearsing is that it is beneficial in several ways. Rehearsals:

- allow us to experiment with the actual words that we are going to use
- allow us to calculate the actual duration of our presentation
- act as a quality-check on our cue cards (or other prompts)

- allow us to check that the presentation area is arranged to our liking
- allow us to gain feedback from an unthreatening audience (even if this is only one person)
- help us to 'learn' the presentation.

The more important the presentation, the more rehearsal is needed, particularly if yours is one of a group of linked presentations and the other presenters are unaware of what you are going to say.

The logistics of a rehearsal

You have to be well prepared to make the best use of your rehearsal time. Below is an agenda that, if you follow it, will ensure that yours are effective rehearsals:

- Prepare the room/space.
- Prepare your visual aids.
- Prepare your 'audience'.
- Prepare yourself.
- Run through the complete presentation.
- Debrief.
- Fine-tune.
- Rehearse the beginning and the end again.
- If you have time, run through the whole thing again.

Rehearsal considerations

Make sure that you have enough time. If your presentation is meant to take 20 minutes, allow at least twice that for the rehearsal. Try to rehearse in the same place that you are going to use for the presentation. This gives you the chance to check that all the kit is working and that the audience seating is comfortable and not crowded, and also the chance to experiment with different places to stand.

If possible, ask a friend who knows both the subject and the expected audience to act as a mock audience. Position all your slides, visual aids and notes or cue cards in exactly the places that they will be during the presentation. If you have arranged for someone to put the slides into the projector or to change the slides for you, make sure that that person attends too – he or she will need the practice. Check that the lighting is suitable: does the room have to be darkened for the slides, and are there any lights glaring into your eyes? Check any sound equipment that you might be using and any cabling that snakes across the presentation area. If there are any loose cables, then either cover them up or stick them down with masking tape.

Tell your mock audience what you want them to look out for. For example, if you worry about either gabbling or speaking too slowly, agree on some sort of signal that will warn you to slow down or speed up, as appropriate. Ask your 'audience' to keep a record of how long the presentation takes, and also to write down any questions that occur to them as you are talking.

Get your first slide ready, take a deep breath and start the rehearsal.

Try to go all the way through without stopping. Don't worry if you hesitate or stumble at first; this is only to be expected. After all, you have never spoken these sentences before, so you should not expect to be word perfect.

When you come to the end, make a note of the time and then go into the debriefing session.

What to look for in the debriefing

This is an opportunity to ask yourself a whole series of questions designed to help you tighten up your presentation.

- What parts were the most successful, and why? This gives you pointers about how you can correct the less successful parts.
- What parts were the least successful, and why? How will you make them better?
- What questions did you raise in the audience's mind? Do you need to alter your presentation to take account of these?
- Do you have any nasty personal habits (twitching, scratching, sniffing and swaying, to name but a few)?
- Was anything superfluous to the presentation?
- Was anything missing?

After the debriefing

Now make any necessary corrections to the cue cards and put down any reminders that might help. (I have a friend who becomes uncharacteristically shy when presenting, so he draws little eyes and smiley faces on his cards to remind him to appear more cheerful and look at the audience more.)

Now run through the start of the presentation again, remembering to project both your voice and your enthusiasm for the subject. Then run through the finish of the presentation, doing the same.

The reason for separately practising the start and finish is that you need to feel really secure about these. The start and finish are the sections of the presentation where it is particularly important to look at the audience, and not to desperately consult your notes.

If you have time, you should run through the whole thing again.

If this all seems like a great deal of effort, well it is, but a good rehearsal will iron out many of the wrinkles that make you feel uncertain when presenting to a real audience. I believe that a thorough rehearsal is one of the best cures for stage fright that I know!

If you really don't have the time for a full rehearsal, at least run through your presentation in front of a mirror. This will give you feedback from yourself while still giving you a chance to practise your actual words.

Voice production and breathing

There is a difference between the way we use our voices in a one-to-one conversation and in a presentation. In ordinary conversation we do not normally have to project our voices. In a presentation we have to ensure that everyone in the room can hear what we are saying, not just the people close to us.

A great deal of research has been done into what annoys people most in a presenter; time and time again the inability to hear what is being said comes top of the list. This means not only that the volume of your voice has to be correct, but also that you should speak at the right speed and articulate your words clearly. The majority of business presentations do not have the advantage of sound enhancement, so you are forced to rely on your voice alone.

If you think that you are a bit weak in this area, then here are some exercises to help you with volume and articulation.

Breathing exercises

Feeling nervous does some horrible things to the way we stand and breathe. Poor posture and breathing lead to poor sound-production, so you need to fix these things first.

● Straighten your back and let your shoulders relax. Lift your hands to waist height, link them loosely and take a really deep breath. Let the breath out with an explosive sigh and then breathe in deeply again. Have your shoulders lifted? If they have, then let them relax again.

- Now hum your breath out:

  Mmmmmmmmmmmmmmmmmmmmmmm

  Try to get as much resonance as you can and make the sound so loud that you make your lips tingle.

- Breathe deeply again, let your shoulders relax and say:

  Aaaaaaaaaaaaaaaaaaaaaaaaaaaaaaaah

  Try to make your voice deep and resonant as you do this.

- Breathe deeply again, let your shoulders relax and mix the two exercises:

  Mmmmaaaaaammmmmaaaaaammmmaaaaah

If your voice seems scratchy, or you have difficulty with the volume, take a sip of water and try again. You may be surprised how much effort it takes to make your voice resonant.

Articulation exercises

Once you have warmed up your lungs and voice-box, you need to limber up your lips and tongue. Poor articulation is due to laziness in the way we pronounce our words. There are several sounds in particular that we are often lazy about. They are the plosive sounds of these letters:

  P   B   T   D   K   G

Lack of clear enunciation of these sounds is especially common when they occur at the ends of words. If you lay extra stress on these sounds it will make your speech much more precise and authoritative. Try the following exercises.

Tongue-twisters

Speak each tongue-twister slowly and distinctly at first; then speed up a little, making sure that you do not drop the ends of the words.

  Before you orate, deliberate and speak your words quite cleanly.

  Mind your Ps and Ts and Ds and speak all plosives keenly.

  Little bottles make clinking rattles when drinking bumpers of port and lemon.

  Don't do what I do, just do what I say.

Teeter totter pitter patter toddle doddle tweedle dee.

Clear articulation not only makes you sound as if you know what you are talking about, it also (if you have a tendency to gabble) slows your speaking speed to a comprehensible level.

Nerves

No book on presentations would be complete without a word or two on stage fright and nerves.

Why do we become nervous before a presentation? We worry about performing badly. We worry that the audience may be hostile. We worry that we will forget our words. We worry that the audience will know more about the subject than we do. We worry that we are about to put ourselves into an exposed position and that people will be judgemental about us. We worry that we have not prepared adequately. In actuality, the chance of any of these things being true is very slim. But nonetheless we feel nervous.

Nervousness shows itself in one or more of the following behaviours:

- Our hands tremble, our voices tremble, and we do not know what to do with our hands, legs, notes, pointer or slides.
- Our pulse becomes faster, our mouth becomes dry and our breathing becomes shallow and rapid.
- We feel the need to protect ourselves from all the eyes looking at us, so we put a barrier between ourselves and the audience by either folding our arms or hunching our shoulders, or even both.
- We want to hide from the audience, so we put a desk or a lectern between us and them. We use our notes as a shield. We clasp or wring our shaking hands tightly.
- We do all we possibly can to avoid looking at the audience by looking instead at the ground, the ceiling, the projector screen or any piece of furniture that does not threaten us.

We feel, in fact, a wreck. But do you know a surprising thing? Nervousness does not show nearly as much as we think.

The first step in handling our nervousness is to confront our unrealistic fears. Table 2 on page 24 will help you to put things into a realistic perspective.

Table 2

DEALING WITH NERVES

What is the most awful thing that could happen to me?	How could I ameliorate this or stop it happening?
I'll perform badly.	Rehearse until you *know* that you can do the presentation reasonably well.
I'll lose my place and forget what I'm supposed to say.	Use your cue cards or speaker's notes.
The audience will be hostile.	Show that you understand their concerns. Realise that they will not be hostile to you personally.
The audience will know more about the subject than I do.	Remember: they have come to the presentation to hear *your* interpretation of the facts.
People will be judgemental about me.	No more judgemental than you are about them.
I shan't have prepared enough.	Oh, yes you will have: think of all that audience research, preparation and rehearsal that you will have done.
The machinery will break down.	Have a back-up strategy. Check the machinery before you start.
My voice will shake.	Breathe out and then breathe in slowly and deeply.
I'll feel exposed.	Plant a friend in the audience and ask him or her to smile and nod encouragingly.
There won't be any questions.	Tell your friend what to ask you when question time starts.
I'll be nervous through the whole presentation.	Oh, no you won't. Nerves always wear off after five minutes or so.

There are several physical things that you can do before a presentation to help you to control your initial stage fright. Most of them, as you will see, you should do on your own before you go into the presentation room:

- Always take a few calm minutes before you present when you can breathe deeply and let your shoulders relax.
- Run cold water over the back of your hands and wrists to cool yourself down.

- Yawn and stretch, then move your jaw around vigorously, screw up your face and then relax it. Blow through your lips like a horse. This stops your face from feeling frozen.
- Put a little colourless lipsalve on the inside of your lips and bite down gently on the sides of your tongue to stop dryness of the mouth.
- Shake your hands and arms vigorously.
- Once in the presentation room, sit straight in your seat while you are waiting to go on. Don't slump, because this hampers your breathing and will cause you to breathe shallowly.
- Always remember: you never look as nervous as you feel!

Now you are ready for the presentation itself. All your hard work is about to come to fruition.

5

 **Delivering the Presentation**

Begin at the beginning and go on till you come to the end; then stop.

Lewis Carroll (1832–98)

The last few minutes before the presentation

Think about how you are going to make your entrance. If you are already seated among the audience, make sure that you are sitting very straight in your chair. Take a slow, deep breath, let your shoulders relax, and then calmly and confidently make your way up to the presentation area. If you are waiting in the wings (so to speak), straighten your back, take a slow, deep breath, let your shoulders relax and walk confidently to the presentation area. Take your time about this, and also take your time making sure that you arrange your slides, notes and anything else that you need in such a way that it is easy for you to pick them up and put them down. This short time while you are preparing the presentation area gives the audience a chance to get used to you: milk it for all it is worth!

If there are any bits and pieces left over from the previous presentation, tidy them away. If the slide projector has to be put in place or the flip chart positioned, take your time about it. You do not want to look flustered or hurried at this point. Make sure that your first visual aid is ready. The calmer and more organised you are now, the calmer you will be when you start the presentation.

When everything is ready and to your satisfaction, take up your position and really look at the audience. This is the 'overture and curtain-up'; if you handle it well the audience will be alert and ready to hear what you have to say. Keep looking at everyone in the audience, give them all a smile, and begin confidently.

Delivering the presentation

If you have rehearsed well and warmed up your lungs and lips, your first words will come out clearly and with authority. Try not to look at your prompt cards during your first few sentences. Indeed, you should not need to at this point (although it is surprising how many people are called Mr/Ms/Mrs Er – as in, 'Good morning, ladies and gentlemen, my name is er...').

There is always a tendency to speak too quietly or too quickly at the start of a presentation, so you must make a real effort not to mumble or gabble your words. Keep the eye contact with the audience high throughout the presentation. High eye contact with the audience shows that you are interested in their response and that what you are saying is truthful. Even if you feel uncomfortable looking into their eyes, force yourself – your credibility depends on this.

Posture and gesture

Stand straight, without bending, twisting or rocking, and keep both feet firmly on the ground. Don't minimise your body size by standing with your feet tightly together and your arms tightly at your sides with your shoulders hunched forward; this posture makes you look as if you would rather not be there. Instead, stand with your feet slightly apart and your hands held together lightly above your waist. It also helps if you lightly hold your cue cards or a pencil. Don't be worried about moving around the presentation area. Unless this is overdone, the audience will welcome the change in position, because it can be quite soporific to give the whole presentation from the same place.

Keep your hands in sight while presenting; if you put them in your pockets or lock them behind your back, you are limiting your ability to gesture. The most successful gestures are the ones you make upwards and outwards towards the audience. (Beware of pointing, though: this can look very aggressive.)

When you need to change a slide or write on a flip chart, keep quiet while you are doing so: addressing your words to the projector or flip chart does not increase your chances of being heard. The whole presentation must be directed at the audience, so face the front at all times. The only reason to look at the screen is to check that the slides are focused and centred – and even then only a quick glance is needed.

Pauses, volume and pace

If you deliver the whole presentation at the same pace you will lull the audience to sleep. When you introduce a new subject or move from one main point to another, signal this by pausing, then raising your voice slightly when you speak again, and perhaps changing position within the presentation area. When you make a really important point, slow down a little and stress each word. Think of your presentation as a symphony – which are the slow movements? What is the theme tune? Where are the recapitulations? How will people know when the symphony has finished?

Audience-watching

Your audience will give you a great many clues to how the presentation is succeeding. If they look serious, that is a good sign, so don't worry about it or feel that you have to make them smile. Nodding is also a very good sign, as are raised eyebrows and a change from relaxed to upright posture. The danger signs, however, are:

- frowning, which betokens puzzlement (you should explain again)
- looking at the door or out of the window, which betokens a desire to leave (so get to the point as quickly as possible)
- a bewildered glance at the ceiling, which may indicate that that person needs a picture or a diagram to understand fully what you are saying.

Throughout the presentation keep checking the audience's reaction, so that if you get a really positive or negative signal from someone you can react to it after the presentation and find out what that person was thinking.

Bringing the curtain down

As you come to your summary and the close of the presentation, make an extra effort to keep your voice up. As I said before, it is tempting to hurry along to question time and, with it, the end of the presentation. After you have taken questions, make your absolutely final remarks as arresting as possible. Deliver them slowly, wait a moment, and then leave the stage with as much dignity as when you came on. If you get it right you may even get a round of applause!

6

Handling the Question-and-Answer Session

There aren't any embarrassing questions – just embarrassing answers.

Carl Rowan

Handling the question-and-answer session

At the end of every successful presentation there should be a question-and-answer session. After all, the audience has sat patiently through your presentation, and now it is their turn to speak.

Inexperienced presenters are often wary of this session, feeling that they might come under fire – that the audience might be out to get them. This very rarely happens. If you have shown throughout the presentation that you have the audience's concerns at heart, then they will see you as a positive source of information and someone whom they can trust.

This does not mean, though, that you can completely relax and pass control over to the audience. The golden rule to remember about a question-and-answer session is this:

YOU DO NOT HAVE TO ANSWER EVERY SINGLE QUESTION;

IT IS UP TO YOU WHICH QUESTIONS YOU CHOOSE TO ANSWER.

On the positive side, a well-handled question-and-answer session offers the presenter several real benefits:

- Because you are not working from a script, your answers seem more off the cuff, and therefore more believable.
- The questions will reflect the overall logic and clarity of your presentation. If there have been (heaven forbid) any sections of your presentation that were not clear, you now have a chance to correct misunderstandings.
- The audience has a chance to gain greater insights into those parts of your presentation that particularly affect them.

- By asking a question, the listener is beginning the process of internalising and so remembering the points that you have made.
- The questions will give you a chance to reinforce yet again the main points of your presentation.

Are there any pitfalls in a question-and-answer session? Well, no interaction between two people can ever be completely predictable, so you have to bear the following things in mind:

- Enthusiastic questioners may want you to reply in such detail that there is a chance of boring the rest of the audience with long answers.
- You may get questions that are not particularly related to the scope of the presentation. Answering these will dilute the impact of your presentation. You should never introduce new topics at this point.
- Some questions may be more like a statement than a question. In such instances the questioner is actually saying, 'Look what I know about the subject too...' rather than really asking a question.
- Once in a blue moon you may get hostile questions, when the questioner has a personal axe to grind and wants to air his or her grievances.

Both the positive and possibly negative aspects of questions should be handled with care. There are two ways of doing this:

- You can put in some feed-forward controls before you start the session.
- You can handle the questions in a disciplined manner.

Let's now look at both these methods.

Feed-forward controls

This is where you set limits to the session:

- You can limit the time: 'We only have time for three or four questions...'
- You can limit the scope of the questions: 'Because time is short, we shall be taking questions only on the financial aspects of this proposal...'
- You can limit the questioners: 'I would now like to take questions from the support staff who will be using these products...'
- You can take only written questions. In this case you should tell the audience at the start of the presentation that this is the case, and then have a short adjournment while you decide which of the questions you are or are not going to handle.

- You can use a master or mistress of ceremonies to run the session. He or she (well briefed by you, of course) will then decide which questions are to be handled.

Question-handling

You have three options here: You can answer then and there; you can defer the answer until after the presentation; you can refuse to answer.

Let's take a look at the types of question that might arise:

- *clarification* questions – 'Can you tell me more about...?'
- *technical* or *detailed* questions – 'What's the specification for...?'
- *peripheral* questions – 'When I was in India, I had an interesting experience...'
- *anticipatory* questions – 'Will you be talking about...?'
- *minefield questions* – 'I've been investigating your claims and...'.

Table 3 will give you some pointers on what you could do:

Table 3
QUESTION-HANDLING

Type of question	Presenter's response
Clarifying	Always answer these. This is a perfect chance to reinforce your message.
Technical/detailed	Answer these if you can keep your answer brief and you know that the answer interests the majority of the audience; otherwise defer the answer until after the presentation.
Peripheral	This depends on who is rambling on. If it is the customer or someone greatly senior to yourself, let them ramble; otherwise let them make their point, politely thank them, and then turn to the rest of the audience and ask, 'Do we have any questions from...?'
Anticipatory	These are lovely if you are going to cover these points: they give you a chance to provide a trailer for the following session. If you are not going to cover them, defer the answer.
Minefield	Don't answer these! Firmly state that you are not prepared to answer, explaining that such matters are outside the remit of the presentation or that the latter is simply not the appropriate time or place.

Question-handling technique

Firstly, it is important that you listen all the way through whatever question is put to you. We all have a tendency to listen only to the start of the question before we busily start working out what our response will be – in effect, we stop listening. This means that our answers are often based only on the first part of the question, not on its entirety.

Having listened attentively to the whole question, you can use the DRAT method of answering:

D Decide whether you are going to answer, defer or refuse the question. If you intend to defer or refuse, say so.

R Rephrase or repeat the question. This allows the rest of the audience to hear it.

A Answer the question briefly and clearly.

T Thank the questioner.

Using a careful methodology for answering questions will give you a feeling of control, so that if anything difficult should occur, you know how to handle it.

One particularly effective way of keeping the question-and-answer session positive is to show that you really have listened to the question and appreciate the chance to answer. Phrases like, 'That's an interesting angle...' or 'I'm glad you asked that...' validate the questioner, give you time to think about your answer and encourage others in the audience to put their questions forward.

Drawing the presentation to a close

When the question-and-answer session is over, you need to draw the presentation to a close. Take your time over this. After all, you only have three more actions to complete: you should summarise your main points again; you should remind the audience of any outcomes from the presentation; and you should leave the presentation area gracefully.

A final visual aid summarising all your points can give you a framework for the first two actions. Keep your summary and action-statements brief, but use emphasis and enthusiasm to put them across.

Leaving the stage gracefully presents more of a problem. You are torn on the one hand between breathing a sigh of relief because it is all over and dashing for the safety of the wings, and on the other recognising the need to signal clearly and calmly that you have ended.

Here are a few ideas:

- Finish your presentation with an upwards and outwards gesture and a farewell statement of some kind: 'So, until we meet again, I wish you all a safe journey home. Good afternoon.'
- Move on to the next activity: 'We shall now adjourn to our working groups to decide on the next course of action.'
- Introduce the next speaker: 'That concludes my presentation. I would now like to introduce Mr Smith, who will be giving the next presentation.'
- Tell the audience where they can contact you: 'That concludes my presentation. I am available for the next 20 minutes in the foyer next door.'

Whatever you do, don't scuttle off the stage like a frightened crab. Calmly gather together your slides and script, and walk off slowly.

A final word

Business presentations should never stand on their own. They are part of the business cycle and so should move the business cycle forward. As Tom Stoppard says in *Rosencrantz and Guildenstern Are Dead*:

> Every exit is an entry somewhere else.

Further Reading

Here is a list of reference material that I have found particularly useful when preparing and delivering presentations:

I ASIMOV (ed.). *The Giant Book of Facts and Trivia*. London, Magpie Books, 1993.

E BURCH DONALD (ed.). *Debrett's Etiquette and Modern Manners*. London, Pan Books, 1982.

P DICKSON. *The Official Rules*. London, Arrow Books, 1978.

Encyclopaedia of Dates and Events. Teach Yourself Books. London, Hodder and Stoughton, 1976.

SIR E GOWERS. *The Complete Plain Words*. Middlesex, Pelican Books, 1977.

R HYMAN (compiler). *A Dictionary of Famous Quotations*. London, Pan Reference Books, 1983.

M McCALLION. *The Voice Book*. London, Faber and Faber, 1988.

D NICKSON AND S SIDDONS. *Business Communications*. Oxford, Butterworth Heinemann, 1996.

The Penguin Dictionary of Quotations. London, Penguin Books. (Any edition.)

G QUINN. *The Clip Art Book*. New York, Crescent Books, 1994.

Roget's Thesaurus. (The latest edition.)

The Shorter Oxford English Dictionary. Oxford, Oxford University Press. (Any edition.)

D WALLECHINSKY, I WALLACE, A WALLACE. *The Book of Lists*. New York, Bantam Books, 1978.

Other titles in the Training Extras series

The Appraisal Discussion
Terry Gillen

The Appraisal Discussion shows you how to make appraisal a productive and motivating experience for all levels of performer – and help your own credibility in the process! Practical advice is given on:

- assessing performance fairly and accurately
- using feedback, including constructive criticism and targeted praise to improve performance
- handling 'difficult' appraisees
- encouraging and supporting reluctant appraisees
- setting, and gaining commitment to, worthwhile objectives
- avoiding common appraiser problems from inadvertent bias to 'appraiser-speak'
- identifying ways to develop appraisees so they add value to the organisation.

1995 48 pages Paperback ISBN 0 85292 618 9 **£5.95**

Assertiveness
Terry Gillen

Assertiveness will help you feel naturally confident, enjoy the respect of others and easily establish productive working relationships, even with 'awkward' people. It covers:

- understanding why you behave as you do and, when that behaviour is counter-productive, knowing what to do about it
- understanding other people better
- keeping your emotions under control
- preventing others bullying, flattering or manipulating you against your will
- acquiring easy-to-learn techniques that you can use immediately
- developing your personal assertiveness strategy.

1997 56 pages Paperback ISBN 0 85292 677 4 **£5.95**

Constructive Feedback
Roland and Frances Bee

Constructive feedback plays a vital role in enhancing performance and relationships. The authors help you identify when to give feedback, how best to give it, and how to receive and use feedback yourself. They offer sound, practical advice on:

- distinguishing between 'destructive' and 'constructive' criticism
- using feedback to manage better – as an essential element of coaching, counselling, training and motivating your team
- improving your skills by following the Ten Tools of Giving Constructive Feedback
- dealing with challenging situations and people
- eliciting the *right* feedback to highlight your strengths and opportunities for your own development.

1996 48 pages Paperback ISBN 0 85292 629 4 **£5.95**

Customer Care
Frances and Roland Bee

Customer Care will help you understand why caring for your customers is so important; how you can improve the service you offer, and, ultimately, how you can contribute to organisational excellence. Clear, practical guidance is given on how to:

- focus on your customers and the services you provide – both internal and external
- identify your *real* customer needs and how best to meet them
- find out what customers *actually* think of your service or product
- improve communication with your customers – face-to-face, on the telephone or in writing
- turn complaints into opportunities to impress
- monitor, evaluate and continuously improve your customer care.

1995 56 pages Paperback ISBN 0 85292 609 X **£5.95**

Decision Making and Problem Solving
John Adair

Decision Making and Problem Solving explains the key principles for developing your thinking skills and applying them creatively and productively to every challenge. Acknowledged as an international authority on management thinking, Adair combines practical exercises with straightforward guidance on:

- understanding the way your mind works
- adopting a structured approach to reach the best decision
- assessing risk and generating successful options for action
- using brainstorming and lateral thinking to increase your creativity
- creating a personal strategy to become a more effective practical thinker.

1997 56 pages Paperback ISBN 0 85292 691 X **£5.95**

Delegating with Confidence
Jonathan Coates and Claire Breeze

The authors consider why this sensible and essential process is so difficult to achieve. They provide a set of practical guidelines to make it happen – enabling you to develop your team and to ensure flexibility while freeing you to spend more time on key aspects of your job. They cover:

- planning what, to whom and how much to delegate
- preparing and training your staff
- assigning the task and defining the key controls – accountability, authority, and responsibility
- letting go but recognising when – and how little – to intervene
- diffusing conflict through skilful listening and questioning
- using delegation as a learning opportunity for others and yourself
- being delegated to – avoiding 'dumping' and managing from the bottom up.

1996 48 pages Paperback ISBN 0 85292 649 9 **£5.95**

The Disciplinary Interview
Alan Fowler

The Disciplinary Interview will ensure you adopt the correct procedures, conduct productive interviews and manage the outcome with confidence. It offers step-by-step guidance on the whole process, including:

- understanding the legal implications
- investigating the facts
- presenting the management case
- probing the employer's case
- diffusing conflict through skilful listening and questioning
- distinguishing between conduct and competence
- weighing up the alternatives – dismissing or dropping the case; disciplining; and improving performance through counselling and training.

1996 56 pages Paperback ISBN 0 85292 635 9 **£5.95**

Effective Learning
Alan Mumford

Effective Learning focuses on *how* we learn. It gives invaluable insights into how you can develop your portfolio of skills and knowledge by managing and improving your ability to learn – positively and systematically. Practical exercises and clear guidance are given on:

- recognising the importance of 'achieved' learning
- understanding the learning process – the Learning Cycle and learning style preferences
- taking best advantage of learning opportunities
- creating and implementing a Personal Development Plan
- encouraging and managing a learning culture.

1995 48 pages Paperback ISBN 0 85292 617 0 **£5.95**

Making Meetings Work
Patrick Forsyth

Making Meetings Work will maximise your time (both before and during meetings), clarify your aims, improve your own and others' performance, and make the whole process rewarding and productive – never frustrating and futile. The book is full of practical tips and advice on:

- drawing up objectives and setting up realistic agendas
- deciding the 'who, where and when' to meet
- chairing effectively – encouraging discussion, creativity, and sound decision-making
- sharpening your skills of observation, listening, and questioning to get across your points
- dealing with problem participants
- handling the follow-up – turning decisions into action.

1995 48 pages Paperback ISBN 0 85292 637 5 **£5.95**

Persuasive Reports and Proposals
Andrew Leigh

Persuasive Reports and Proposals will ensure that what you write gets the results that you want. It covers five crucial aspects which spell out PRIDE – what you should feel about your documents if they are to win hearts and minds:

- *Purpose* – clarifying your aim and constructing a persuasive argument
- *Reader* – identifying and understanding your audience to anticipate objections and retain attention
- *Image* – creating an appropriate style and tone while avoiding spoilers (poor grammar, literals etc) which undermine credibility
- *Detail* – using effective facts, logical links and simple sentences
- *Enhancers* – seeking commitment, building in emotional appeal and editing to perfect your draft.

1997 56 pages Paperback ISBN 0 85292 676 6 **£5.95**

Telephone Skills
Patrick Forsyth

This book sets out simple principles and techniques to enhance your communication skills and ensure you make a positive impact with every ring! It covers:

- taking calls – initial impressions, projecting the right individual and corporate image
- making calls – deciding what you want to achieve, establishing rapport and getting your message across
- using your voice, intonation and language to best effect
- listening attentively and knowing when to take the initiative
- diffusing anger and winning over difficult callers
- exceeding customer expectations and leaving a lasting impression.

1997 48 pages Paperback ISBN 0 85292 674 X **£5.95**

Writing Job Descriptions
Alison Hardingham

Writing Job Descriptions guides you systematically through the whole process, ensuring your job descriptions are clear and accurate and make a positive contribution to key management tasks. Practical help is given on:

- deciding what to do with full-length examples for both simple and more complex jobs
- defining essential job constituents
- maintaining flexibility while avoiding contractual difficulties
- using job descriptions to increase the effectiveness of your recruitment, selection, induction and appraisal procedures
- tailoring the information to assist in job evaluation.

1997 48 pages Paperback ISBN 0 85292 692 8 **£5.95**